It's All In your mind, James Robert

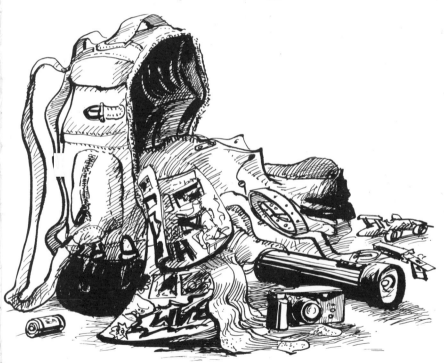

Written by Rebecca Weber
Illustrated by Mike Spoor

To Winifred Howard,
who told me about the real James Robert.

Written by Rebecca Weber
Illustrated by Mike Spoor

© 1995 Shortland Publications Inc.

04 03 02 01 00 99
11 10 9 8 7 6 5 4

Published by Shortland Publications Inc.

Distributed in the United States of America by

a division of Reed Elsevier Inc.
500 Coventry Lane
Crystal Lake, IL 60014
800-822-8661

Distributed in Canada by

PRENTICE HALL GINN
1870 Birchmount Road
Scarborough
Ontario M1P 2J7

Printed through Bookbuilders Limited, Hong Kong.

ISBN: 0-7901-0989-1

CONTENTS

CHAPTER 1

And they call it a mountain! Yes, it's true, not even the great Everest itself was a match for the daring mountaineer, Nick Danger. From its dizzy height, Danger looked out across the glorious landscape. His perch was precarious at best, but hanging onto a boulder at the top of the world was child's play compared to the path he had just blazed across the previously uncharted rock-face of the mountain. No easy, mapped-out route for him! In fact, Danger's climbing companions – the best in the world – had thought it madness to follow him. So he had done it alone, relying on his muscles, his cunning, and his trusty ice ax. His booming laugh echoed across the valley – he was Nick Danger, "King of the Mountain!"

"James Robert Howard! I have called you six times now! Would you please stop laughing like a maniac, climb out of that tree, and come in for dinner."

Jim looked down at the impatient figure waiting below. "Sorry, Mom," he said sheepishly, embarrassed at having been overheard. "I'll be right there."

As he slid down, Jim felt a branch snag his shirt. Great. If Mom was already irritated, a ripped shirt could really set her off.

Mom looked very serious. "You know, mister, I'm hungry enough that if you hadn't heard me, I'd have gone up there after you and brought you down myself!"

Jim looked up just in time to catch her big, slow wink. He started to chuckle. Yeah, his mom was all right. Sometimes, she really seemed to remember what it was like to be ten years old.

As they walked into the kitchen together, Mom started to laugh. Dad was wearing an apron and dancing around the kitchen with a roast chicken on a big platter.

"Dad!" Jim was mortified. "Mom, do something..." But before the words were even out of his mouth, Mom had left him and run to meet his dad. She curtseyed, took his free hand, and started to dance around with him. Jim started laughing in spite of himself. No, it wasn't just his mom who remembered what it was like to be a kid – his dad was just as bad!

Later, empty plates pushed back, Jim turned to his dad. "Hey, Pop, guess what!

Mom thought she could climb that tree out back. Isn't that a riot?"

"Oh, Jim, Jim, Jim." Dad shook his head. "You're underestimating your mom. You should hear what your uncles say about her when she was your age. She was the biggest adventurer on her block!"

Mom was looking as dignified as possible. "I don't know what you're talking about. Adventurer! I was as serious as they come!" But the twinkle in her eyes belied every word she said.

Suddenly, she pushed back her chair. "Speaking of being serious, we have some serious work to do. Everybody move it! We've got to get everything cleaned up and finish packing for tomorrow, or we'll never make it out of here."

Jim groaned to himself. His family was leaving on vacation tomorrow. No wonder his parents were acting so hyper – they couldn't wait to "get away from it all" and head off to the wilderness. Jim, on the other hand, was not excited at all. Being the son of the world's biggest fresh-air fiends was not all it was cracked up to be. They were always carting him off to crazy places in the middle of nowhere, and he was always the only kid around for miles.

He didn't even like camping. Jim knew he was the worst boy scout in the troop. He could never pay attention during all those explanations on how to build a shelter out of tree branches, or how to make a rabbit trap out of a shoelace. He'd really *try* to listen, but the next thing he knew, he'd start thinking about what it would have been like to be a famous explorer, and...

"Come on, Jim, help me with the dishes." Mom smiled at him. "Then I'll come up and help you get everything together for our trip. I think you're going to love where we're going – who knows, maybe you'll have a few adventures of your own!"

Jim pushed back his chair slowly. "Adventures?" he said to himself. "Yeah, right. Whoever heard of a real kid having a real adventure?"

CHAPTER 2

Could he stand the pain any longer? He had known there would be tremendous pressure in the cockpit – traveling across dry salt flats at speeds of well over 350 mph will do that to you. But he, Sam Speed, world-renowned Formula One racing champion, had never imagined this. His lips, white and bloodless, were pulled back from his teeth in a horrifying grin by the force... his hands, throbbing and stiff, were barely able to control his jet-propelled machine... even his heart, beating madly, irregularly, was just trying to survive a challenge for which no frail, human body is really equipped. Yet, Speed knew that if he could travel at twice the speed of sound, the test would be a success. He would be a hero...

" James Robert!" His mom turned to his dad. "You see, dear, he's doing it again – look at that horrible face he's making. That imagination of his just starts running away with him, and he doesn't even have a clue what's happening around him." She looked at her son again. "Jim!"

"What? I've been listening... uh, what is it?" Jim scrambled to collect his thoughts, just like he was always having to do in school – or boy scouts – whenever his teacher realized he wasn't paying attention.

"I was just wondering what your opinion was about where we should stay," said Mom. "Your dad and I have been listening to the radio, and it looks like the wilderness area that we were planning to go to has already had about three inches of rain in the past day or so, and another big storm is moving in."

"Oh... so we're going home?" Jim couldn't believe his luck!

"No!" Mom was getting exasperated. "We're still going to the park, but instead of sleeping in tents, we were thinking of staying in one of the cabins that the park rents out to tourists. What we wanted to know is if that would be something *you'd* like to do."

"Sure, Mom, the cabins sound good," Jim said. He figured he'd better try a little harder. "But if the weather gets better, let's try the tents. That's really the whole reason we go, isn't it?" His effort paid off – Mom gave him one of her best smiles.

Dad also seemed pleased. "Hey, slugger, how about showing us some of those hot tricks you've been learning in boy scouts? We're going to need your expertise, especially when we try to build a fire tonight – the wood's going to be soaked!" He laughed heartily. Jim smiled weakly. No, a little rain wouldn't turn back *his* family – in fact, it didn't look like the rain could even dampen his dad's enthusiasm.

Jim turned and looked back out of the window at the landscape racing by. While he had been daydreaming, they had traveled from the dry, grassy plains he was familiar with to rainy, tree-covered mountains. "This is getting worse," he thought miserably to himself. "Not only do I have to camp, I have to figure out how to do it without drowning!"

Several hours later, the family pulled into a small cluster of cabins. Dad stepped out of the car and stretched. "This air even *tastes* good!" he exclaimed, waving his arms in big circles. "Come on, guys, get out here – you can even smell the ocean!"

"Honey, I think you're probably just smelling the rain," smiled Mom, "but it really is glorious. Come on, Jim! Whoops – watch that big puddle there!"

Jim's first step into the wilderness had landed him directly into a deep patch of mud that promptly oozed into his shoe. He forced a big, completely unfelt smile. "Mom, where did you say you packed my hiking boots?" he asked with extreme patience.

Jim's spirits started to rise, however, when they walked into the cabin. It was dark and smelled musty, but it had a giant stone fireplace and, best of all, a big loft. He promptly climbed the ladder, and, on reaching the top, called down, "Hey, can I sleep up here? It's really cool!"

He started to explore without waiting for an answer. The loft had a beamed, sloping roof, which, Jim thought, would be a lot less likely to leak rain on his head than his tent. There was also a large window that looked out over the roof of the back porch, directly into the dark, wet forest. "Okay, so the view isn't that great," he said, "but this is the best place we've ever camped!"

"Hello, there!" a strange voice called out. "Hate to barge in, but my wife and I saw you folks pull up and thought we'd just say howdy." A large, bearded man in a lumberjack shirt and a gray cowboy hat had poked his head in the front door. "This here rain's been keeping all but us diehards away, so it's nice to see we've finally got us some neighbors."

Jim's mother stepped forward, extending her hand. "Pleased to meet you! We're the Howards... You mean, we're the only two families here right now?"

"Yup! Oh, exceptin' Mrs. Forrest – she's that little ol' gal who rented you this spread, and she lives up in that there front unit. Oh, and I'm Buck Weston, from Montana. Well, darned if I didn't fergit why I'm here! Marge – that's my wife – and I wanted to know if you'd come and have a bite of supper with us tonight. It's jest the two of us, and we're feeling lonesome as a couple of polecats!"

No kids. Jim went back over to his sleeping bag. Well, it looked like his parents were going to have some friends here, but not him. So much for having any adventures – what was one kid going to do by himself?

CHAPTER 3

They were headed into battle! The salty wind whipped and stung the old pirate's craggy, weather-beaten face, as his eyes searched the waves for the enemy ship. Running low on supplies, men ready to mutiny after months of hunger and backbreaking work, his own almost inhuman strength starting to wane after days and nights of constant watching and guiding – despite these things, Bartholomew the Brave still knew they would succeed, and succeed with glory. They were going to track down his evil nemesis, Peter the Polluter of the Pacific, and reclaim the treasures stolen from many nations. That would put an end, once and for all, to the nightmare of war at sea. They just needed to hurry. "Faster!" he bellowed to his men, "Faster...!"

"James Robert!" said Mom, embarrassed. "Your dad and Mr. Weston are sailing as fast as they can – you don't need to yell at them. And please sit down – you're going to tumble out if you stand at the front of the boat!"

"Well, now, we call that the "bow" out here on the high seas, ma'am," said Mr. Weston, grinning at Jim. "And I don't think a fella should mind a bit of enthusiasm! I'm gettin' anxious to see those sea lions myself!"

Jim smiled back at him. Dinner last night had turned out OK. Despite being just as nature-crazed as his parents, the Westons were both really nice, and seemed to be just as interested in seeing that Jim had a good time as the adults. In fact, it had been Mrs. Weston who suggested this boat trip.

"Well, I'm just about dog-tired of all this talk about big ol' mountain peaks and purty valleys," she had said the night before, with a slight nod toward Jim. "How about we do something with a little more kick to it?" Jim, filled up with stew and biscuits, and mesmerized by the blazing fire, was suddenly alert. "What would you folks say to a little ocean roundup?" she asked.

So here they were. Dad and Mr. Weston had rented a sailboat, and now they were sailing up the coast toward a herd of sea lions, famous in the area for their friendliness.

Jim was enjoying every minute of the trip. He had never been to the ocean before, and its salty smell and brisk breeze were just as thrilling to him as anything his imagination had ever invented. From his perch on the bow, he spotted the herd first.

"There they are – there are hundreds of them!" he yelled. "Check it out, there are even babies out here swimming." He leaned farther over the rail to get as close as he could to the sea lions, now swarming up to the boat.

Jim's parents smiled at one another. In spite of, or maybe *because* of, the weather, this vacation was turning out much better than they had hoped. "Hey, Jim," called out his dad, "that little one really seems to like you! Look at how he's swimming up to you – and you thought you wouldn't find any friends!"

A small sea lion, only half the size of the others, had moved up very close to the boat, and was bobbing up as high as he could to get near Jim's hand. "I think he just wants to chew on one of my fingers," Jim laughed, but the sea lion really did seem very friendly.

Suddenly, his little friend disappeared! Another, much larger sea lion had swum up and right over the baby to get near the boat. Jim jerked his hand back fast – this big guy really meant business!

"Well now, there you go," said Mr. Weston. "That's what happens when folks get to feedin' these critters. They see a boat, and they run up all frenzied, like a bunch of hogs at slop time! It ain't right – they'll just get lazy and have a harder time makin' a go of it themselves." He shook his head sadly.

Jim was only half-listening. He was absolutely hypnotized by the sea lions. He had seen pictures of them in the school encyclopedia before; but in those photos, they had just looked big and blubbery. Here, in real life, they were sleek, graceful, and athletic. Having an audience didn't seem to bother them at all. In fact, if anything, it turned them into bigger clowns, as they leaped about and played together in the dark green water.

Jim's mom joined him. "They make it look easy, don't they? It almost makes you want to jump in there with them..." She looked enviously at the water.

"No kidding! Unfortunately, I think we'd freeze to death in about two minutes – that water is cold! On top of *that*, that big guy down there would sink us in a second."

The giant sea lion responded with a flip of his tail that sent a shower of cold water cascading over the boat and onto its passengers. Their laughter was cut short as the boat gave a sudden violent lurch!

The storms, which had cleared away that morning, were back and stronger than ever. Angry black clouds had filled the sky, unnoticed by the boat's occupants engrossed in watching the sea lions, and strong gusts of wind were now blasting across the water.

"We've got to get going – NOW!" yelled Mr. Weston to Jim's father.

The rest of the passengers, who had gone quiet, scurried to their places. Mom rushed to control the mainsail, the boom of which was lashing around dangerously, while Dad and Mr. Weston worked frantically to get the boat under control. Mrs. Weston quickly but calmly pulled up the anchor. Together, the four adults got the boat moving in the right direction, headed for the shore.

Jim was frightened – really frightened. The waves that had been calmly lapping against the side of the boat were now roaring, white monsters tossing the little boat around like a nutshell. The entire deck was awash, and Jim held on fiercely to one of the ropes anchoring the sails.

The adults were all occupied in keeping the boat under control, and, as the minutes passed, they pulled closer and closer to shore. Jim slightly relaxed his hold on the rope.

Then, in an instant, his worst nightmare came true. He was underwater! Choking, spluttering, he couldn't see, he couldn't breathe! He flailed his arms and legs around, trying to surface... Then a strong arm yanked him back into the air – he was back on the deck! What had happened?

"Oh, thank you, thank you!" gasped Jim's mom, holding him tightly. "When that wave hit you, I thought you were going under for sure." She hugged him harder, not wanting to let him go.

Jim's dad made his way over, pale as a ghost, and grabbed them both. "Jim, your mom is the bravest person in the world!" he choked. "You should have seen how she reached into that wave to get you!"

Even if Jim had had any breath to speak, he wouldn't have known what to say. He grabbed onto a rope again as tightly as he could, and motioned to his mother to go back and help sail. By now, however, they had reached a more secluded bay, and the little boat was sailing smoothly again.

When they were back safely on the beach, Mr. Weston and his wife came up to Jim. "Son, I'm right proud of you," Mr. Weston began. "You sure were brave out there. You didn't even let out a peep!" Mrs. Weston just smiled warmly at him and squeezed his arm.

But Jim didn't feel very brave. He couldn't talk because he was still scared to death. Yes, he'd had a real adventure, but he hadn't done anything courageous. All of those brave things he was always imagining himself doing were just that, imagination. He'd had to be saved, just like a little kid. His mom was the brave one, not him. He turned and walked slowly up to the cabin.

CHAPTER 4

Yes, the dry heat was a killer – it sapped a man's strength and destroyed his will. Yet, famed archaeologist Mitch Intrepid knew that he must forge ahead if he were to find it. "It" was treasure, unimaginable riches left by a tribe of cannibals that had inhabited this land many years ago. Back then, the area was still a sweltering jungle, for these people had lived long before global warming had turned their home into this inhospitable desert of death. Wiping the sweat out of his eyes, Intrepid looked at the horizon, trying to match his barren surroundings with the jungle landscape shown on the long-dead chieftain's map. He would find the treasure, the fame and glory would be his, because no one else would have the courage, the sheer willpower, the...

Jim stumbled. "Who are you fooling, James Robert Howard?" he said bitterly to himself. "No matter what you make up, you know none of it is even close to the truth. Real adventurers are brave and strong, not weak and scared. Give it up!"

He refocused his eyes on the ground, watching his hiking boots clomp up the path in front of him. His parents were swimming with the Westons in the little secluded bay where they had landed the boat the day before. The storm had spent its fury, leaving behind a hot, muggy day.

Still, Jim didn't want to go in the water. He saw the dark clouds looming low on the horizon – he knew that they would probably bring stormy weather again, and he didn't want to be anywhere near the ocean if they did.

"Well, sure, son, if that's what you really want to do," his dad had said, looking concerned, when Jim had asked if he could go for a hike up into the hills instead of staying on the beach. "Just stick to the trail that we went on the other day. But wouldn't you rather have one of us go with you?"

"No thanks, I kind of want to go alone. You guys go swimming – I'll be OK."

As he walked away, he heard Mr. Weston behind him. "Ya know," he had drawled to Jim's dad, "ya gotta get that boy back up on the horse. Sure, he's a little spooked right now, but he'll get over it. The water's calm as a sleeping kitten today."

Jim walked faster, hoping to be out of sight in case his dad decided to take Mr. Weston's advice. "I don't want to get back up on any old horse," he muttered to himself. "I'm just fine." He kicked at a branch that lay across the path. Then he kicked at a rock, shooting it out in front of him.

He became so intent on kicking the rock that he didn't even notice his path had turned back toward the water. Suddenly, the rock disappeared – it had flown off the top of the small cliff which Jim had unknowingly climbed. He peered over to see where it landed and found himself looking down at another small bay, about half a mile up the coast from where his parents and the Westons were swimming. This bay was choked with weeds and smelled horrible.

"Gross!" thought Jim. He was just turning away when he caught a small movement out of the corner of his eye. He looked more closely and saw something shiny and brown in the water. "Is it a sea lion?"

Ignoring the smell and forgetting his fear of water, he slithered down the sandy cliff to the water's edge and waded in. It was a young sea lion and it was all alone. Thinking it was his friend from yesterday, Jim moved closer.

"What's the matter, little buddy? Did that stupid storm separate you from your family and wash you in here? Is that what happened?" By this time, he had reached the small body in the shallow water. "Why don't you just swim back out?"

Then he saw why the small animal, a different one from yesterday, but still just a baby, wasn't swimming away. It was caught, horribly tangled, in pieces of plastic that had bound its flippers and cut into its skin. Jim was angrier than he had ever been in his life.

He grabbed at the plastic, and broke it, strand by strand. The sea lion was too hurt, or too exhausted, to even struggle. Jim finally was able to pull the last of the plastic away. It had once been a plastic container that held a six-pack of soda. The baby looked up at him, its eyes rolling in terror.

"It's OK, it's OK," breathed Jim, trying to soothe the injured animal. "We've gotten rid of that horrible plastic. You're free! Are you going to be able to swim?" He realized the animal was sensing his anger at the situation, and he tried to calm himself down to keep from frightening it any more.

While he stroked its head, he looked more closely at the little sea lion. There were

definitely welts where the plastic had been,
but the skin was actually broken in only a few
places. "Well, it looks like your blubber saved
you from being hurt too badly."

While he let the sea lion rest, Jim looked around at the water in the bay and was horrified by what he saw. Old, rusty cans bobbed dangerously on the top of the water. Soggy heaps of cardboard lay around the shore and on the ocean floor. Black tires choked one section of the bay. Worst of all, there was a greasy, stinking, disgusting film floating on the water's surface. In fact, the baby sea lion's fur was coated in it.

"I don't think this place is very healthy for either of us, buddy," Jim said. "I know you're not feeling very well, but we've got to get you out of here." He gave the sea lion an encouraging nudge, but it wouldn't move – it was just too scared.

When it had been caught earlier, every movement, no matter how small, had tightened the plastic's deadly hold. The animal had quickly learned that keeping still hurt less. "You poor little guy, you just don't know what to do, do you?" Jim asked kindly.

At that moment, Jim knew it was up to him. Cutting the plastic away was not going to be enough to save this baby animal – if it were left here, it would die for sure.

CHAPTER 5

The ocean can sense fear. If you let it know you are not as brave, as ruthless, as it is, it will never let you escape its grasp. Rick Daring adjusted his goggles and checked that fragile link that kept him alive – the thin rubber air hose leading to his oxygen tank. He was going to do it. He was going to delve deep into the bowels of the earth, searching its murky depths for the lost submarine. He knew the dangers involved, but only by putting himself at the mercy of the water's strength, could he hope to succeed. There! He could sense the submarine ahead of him – he had been right! In the same way that whales communicate with each other hundreds of feet below the surface of the water, he'd listened to the signals the ocean was sending him. And he had succeeded – the lost submarine was found, and its passengers were going to survive!

"It's OK, James Robert Howard, it's OK!" Jim didn't realize he had gone from encouraging the sea lion to encouraging himself as they moved out of the calm waters of the secluded bay. The water was over his waist now, and he could feel the current tugging at his feet.

He had wrapped one of his arms around the sea lion's back and was guiding it away from the choking weeds and polluted water. As they moved into cleaner water, the animal seemed to be regaining some of its strength. It looked a lot more alert than it had before, and the stinking film was washing off quickly in the salty water. "You feel more at home out here, don't you, buddy?" Jim asked the animal, wishing desperately that he did, too.

He wasn't sure that he should release the sea lion, but he was finally forced to by a big rush of water that nearly tipped him over. Even though he had been careful to stay in water no deeper than his shoulders, the waves were bigger out here, and at first he was very close to panicking. Then Jim realized that if he jumped up just as the wave came at him, he could keep his head above the surface.

The sea lion was starting to use its flippers. They were obviously very sore, and at first, it was just as clumsy as Jim was in the waves. Then it started to become more confident, and was soon bobbing very ably around him. There was a loud barking sound close by and the animal perked up its head and answered. A small group of about ten sea lions was swimming out in the calmer waters, away from the waves breaking on the beach.

"Here he is," shouted Jim, knowing very well that they couldn't understand a word he was saying. He didn't care – he felt great, even though the water was starting to seem quite cold. He had been worrying about what was going to become of his friend, because he really didn't think it had any business being alone – the animal was too young to take care of itself. Now it had a chance!

Without looking back, the little sea lion swam off to rejoin its family, and Jim rode a small wave into the beach. It tumbled him end over end, and he got sand in his nose, but it was all OK. He danced around on the beach in his soaking wet clothes. The baby sea lion had needed help, and he, James Robert Howard, had come to the rescue!

He took off his socks and hiking boots to let them dry in the sun. The dark clouds were still hanging over the horizon, but so far, they had not moved in, and the day's warmth felt wonderful after his unexpected swim.

◆ða◆

After awhile, Jim's clothes were nearly dry, and he decided it was time to get back to his own family. He looked at his watch and realized that he had been gone for over two hours – although it seemed like much longer because so much had happened to him. Still, he didn't want his family to worry. "I don't think they'd be very impressed with my adventure," he thought to himself. "Mom might flip if she found out I was messing around with sea lions in the ocean!"

He climbed up the path along the small cliff and jogged back to the beach where he'd left his parents and the Westons. They were all lying on the beach, talking away like old friends. His dad and Mr. Weston were sitting near the path, and his mom and Mrs. Weston were slightly farther up, just out of earshot. His dad looked up concerned, as Jim approached.

"How're you doing, slugger? Did you have a nice walk?" he asked, trying not to let his worry show too much. Mr. Weston glanced at him curiously.

"I sure did, Dad. In fact, you know what I did?" Jim grinned. "I saw a horse along the way, and I got right back up on it!" His dad's forehead wrinkled for a moment, and then a huge smile broke out across his face as he realized that Jim had, by himself, faced and beaten his fear of the ocean. Mr. Weston burst out laughing.

"Son, you beat all!" Mr. Weston gasped. "I didn't think you'd heard me, and I do hope you're not riled at me for being such a busybody, but I think you're A-OK!"

"Wait a minute, Jim," broke in his dad, "I hope you were careful – you know the ocean can be pretty powerful. I don't really like the idea of you swimming in it all by yourself."

"Believe me, I know, Dad. Don't worry, I just did what I had to do – you know I'm not exactly famous for running around, risking my neck."

There. Jim had told the exact truth, even if it was only part of the story. "But," he continued, leaning over and dropping his voice to a whisper, "maybe we'd better not tell Mom – I don't want her to be worried." Mr. Weston started laughing again, and his dad joined in, although somewhat uncertainly.

◆❧◆

That evening, as Jim was changing out of his salty clothes into clean jeans and a sweatshirt, he glanced at his boots. He noticed that the rubber sole on one of them had a deep gouge in it. "I must have stepped on a broken bottle or something in that gross water," he thought to himself. "Boy, I was lucky I was wearing these things!"

Then, as he thought about what might have happened to him if he hadn't been wearing thick boots and trousers, he started to get angry. He remembered that stinking film on the water and the way it had matted the baby sea lion's fur and stuck to his own hands, and he got angrier.

Jim remembered the welts on the sea lion's skin left by the plastic, and the frightened, hopeless expression in the sea lion's eyes when he had found it, and he was absolutely furious.

Steaming mad, he went down to dinner. Luckily, his parents and the Westons were already deep in conversation when he arrived, so they didn't notice or ask him why he was so quiet.

"Well, we think it's worse than a crime," his dad was saying. "No matter how often environmentalists point out the problem, there are too many greedy people out there who just don't care about being responsible when there's money involved!"

Jim pricked up his ears – he couldn't believe the adults were talking about the very thing that had him so upset. He was very familiar with the tone of this conversation. His dad and mom often talked about pollution at home, but he was ashamed to admit he had never really paid much attention.

"Ain't that the truth," agreed Mr. Weston. "Problem is, the big ol' money-grubbers don't take any more notice of what we're saying than a bull takes notice of a fly buzzing 'round its ears. We're too small, and they're too big – we can't hurt 'em!"

"Nonsense!" Jim's mom wasn't going to accept that for a minute. "We just haven't found the right strategy yet. And if you're going to compare us to insects, compare us to something like ants, which can carry loads ten times heavier than their bodies. A group of ants, working together, can move a mountain! Maybe each one of us just needs to carry more than we feel we possibly can at first, and if we all do that together, we will get the job done."

That was his mom! Jim knew that she and his dad both felt very strongly about these issues. In fact, they were always talking about how they had met in college at some sort of a march protesting something or other.

The conversation went back and forth like a tennis match. Jim learned more that night about the problems facing the environment than he had in the rest of his life put together. As he listened, his fiery anger changed to a firm resolve.

For the second time that day, Jim knew that the problem in the bay was his to solve. He had found it, and now he, James Robert Howard, would have to do all he could to find a solution.

CHAPTER 6

The hour had come – the general must make his move now. He had to do it for the sake of his troops, before they ran out of supplies, time, and that most precious commodity of all: courage. General Dirk Victor, the country's youngest five-star general in history, knew the enemy was wily, ruthless, and unforgiving. And they could be anywhere in that leaf-covered countryside. Sending his men into that dank maze would be folly. The enemy would escape in the confusion and emerge on the other side to fight again. No, Victor knew they had to spot the enemy first. Then they could fight. But who should he send on this dangerous, lonely mission? Then Victor remembered the two main rules of war chiefs everywhere: "Never let anyone touch your weapon," and "Never send someone else to do the job you should do yourself." He would go, alone...

"James Robert Howard," Jim hissed to himself, "stop daydreaming! You've got more than enough to think about already!"

But that was the problem. He knew he had to do something, but what? He didn't know who was responsible for the trash dumping, or even how to begin to find out. The problem was so big and so awful that it was completely overwhelming him.

"Maybe I should tell Mom and Dad about this," he thought reluctantly. "Even though they'll probably chew me out for messing around in polluted water and swimming in the ocean alone, they'd at least know what to do next."

He really wasn't crazy about that idea. After all, *he* had been the one to find and help the sea lion – it was the best thing that he'd ever done in his whole life and he wanted to take care of the problem himself. Maybe this is what Mom was talking about when she said that people need to do more than they feel they can.

Before Jim could think about it further, his mom climbed up the ladder to his loft and sat down beside him.

"Honey, would you mind if your dad and I went out with the Westons for awhile tonight?" she asked. "We want to hike up to the top of one of the trails to look at the stars – it's so clear out this evening, it would give us a great chance to watch the sky."

"Sure, Mom… hey, but can I go, too? It sounds really cool!"

"Well, that's the thing. You know how there's that little town down the highway where we rented the boat yesterday? We want to wait and go after most of its lights have gone out, so there's nothing to interfere with the light from the stars. So, we probably won't even be leaving here until around 10:30 or 11:00 p.m." Mom smiled at him. "I'm sorry, Jim, I think it would be great for you, but that's just too late for you to be out."

"I understand," he replied, "that's OK too, though. I'll have fun here by myself – I've got plenty of books to read and a new puzzle to do."

"Um, that's what I really came to tell you about." Mom looked uncomfortable. "You remember Mrs. Forrest, that nice old lady who lives down at the first cabin? Well, she said she would be happy to come up here and stay with you."

"Oh come on, Mom, I'm ten years old – I'm perfectly fine to stay here by myself." After all the adventures Jim had had that day, he felt more responsible than ever before, and now this? Even with *his* imagination, he couldn't think of anything that sounded like less fun.

"I know you are, but it's not as if you're at home," Mom answered. "If something happens, or if you need help, it really is better to have an adult here."

Jim looked at his mom. She really did want to go, he could tell, so he didn't want to ruin it for her. "OK, Mom, but if it's all too boring, can I just tell her I want to come up here and go to bed? Then I can read or mess around up here or something."

"Of course! Thanks, Jim."

It was now 10 p.m. Jim's mom and dad had left for the Weston's nearly an hour ago, and Jim was starting to think about retiring to the loft. Mrs. Forrest was nice enough, but she really was a little strange. Nearly seventy, she had spent most of her life out here in the country, away from civilization and other people. In all those years, she had developed some habits that seemed pretty odd to Jim.

For one thing, she didn't have – and didn't want – a telephone. Jim smiled to himself, remembering how his mom had wanted someone to be there to get help if he needed anything. He would probably know how to do that better than Mrs. Forrest!

Another thing about the old lady, she had very strong opinions about the few people she did come in contact with – she either loved them or hated them. No middle ground for her!

Jim was working on his puzzle, a really complicated one, and having a hard time with it. He remembered his dad's advice about puzzles, and repeated it to himself over and over: "If it's too hard," his dad always said, "just take care of the pieces you know first. Even if you put only two of them together, it still gives you two less to worry about later."

While he was working, he half-listened to Mrs. Forrest's chatter. "And I'll tell you," she was saying, "I don't know where that Frank Conner is getting all that money, but I'll lay you two to one that it isn't on the right side of the law!"

She rocked her chair back and forth furiously. "There he is, driving around in that brand-new car, and rubbing elbows with that snake-in-the-grass, Otto Farnsworth. Yes siree, that Frank Conner's up to no good. He never was, nor was his father before him. A bunch of snakes, that's what they all are!"

"What?" Jim perked up his ears. A couple of local villains, hmm? He decided to pry for a little more information. "So, Mrs. Forrest, do these guys all live around here?"

She looked at him in surprise, almost as if she had forgotten he was there. "Well, Frank Conner and his dad have a run-down old shack not too far from here, although Frank's been bragging about buying some new ritzy place up by the golf course. Where he's going to get the money for *that* I don't know. Those Conners have never had two dimes to rub together before."

"How about that other guy, Otto-somebody?"

"Otto Farnsworth? You haven't heard of Otto Farnsworth? Oh, that's right, you aren't from around here, are you? He owns that big oil refinery not far from here. He's as rich as a king and as mean as a skunk, I can tell you. I wouldn't trust that man as far as I could throw him!"

Dishonest men and an illegal dumping ground. Suddenly, Jim realized that his dad's advice about puzzles applied to real-life puzzles, too. He had his two pieces of information to start with, now he just had to see how they fit together.

"Um, Mrs. Forrest? I'm really tired, would you mind if I went up to my room now?" Jim had to get away and start thinking this through.

CHAPTER 7

The criminal mind is a mystery. In some ways, crooks are clever in their dastardly schemes. But even the most cunning have one fatal flaw: they forget that when they enter the dark world of crime, someone will soon be hot on their heels – and that someone is Dick Tracker, the private eye's private eye. Tracker slouched against the building, pulling the collar of his trench coat up and the brim of his battered fedora down, to hide his noble face, for it was known and feared in the underworld. He watched and waited, like the predator he was, knowing his prey would soon come into sight. He knew their habits well. That's why he always won. "They'll wait until it's dark, thinking that'll hide them," he muttered to himself with a knowing chuckle. "Why are crooks all so unoriginal? They always wait until it's dark..."

"James Robert Howard, I think you've got it!" Jim was excited. Of course, they would wait and dump their disgusting garbage when it was dark! That way, there would be less chance of being seen. And they would also wait for a night like this one – when it's clear and dry, so they could see what they were doing without using flashlights, or searchlights, or anything else that might give them away.

Jim had been looking out of the big window in his room, trying to think of a plan of action ever since he had left Mrs. Forrest an hour ago.

"I'm going to head over to that beach and see if anything's happening," he said to himself, as he moved quietly around his room, tying on his boots, and pulling on a dark sweater that he hoped would camouflage him. He also grabbed his backpack, which had his flashlight in it. "Even though I won't be able to do anything to stop them, maybe I can get some kind of proof of what they're doing to use as evidence against them later."

The thought of evidence reminded him of his parents' camera, with which he had been experimenting earlier that day on the beach. He checked his backpack and was relieved to see it there. "Perfect," he whispered.

Before leaving, he peeked over the banister at Mrs. Forrest. She was sound asleep in her rocking chair below. "If I hurry," he thought, "I should be back long before Mom and Dad come in. No one will ever know I've been away."

Jim climbed out of his window and down the trellis on the back porch, thanking his lucky stars that he had chosen his loft bedroom that first day. He couldn't have been so sure of escaping unnoticed if he'd had to go out of the front door past Mrs. Forrest.

At the bottom, he let his eyes get used to the dark, because he didn't want to use his flashlight unless he absolutely had to.

Jim was so busy trying to keep quiet, and to keep from tripping in the dark, that it took him much longer to get to the beach than he remembered from his previous trip there that day. "I hope I haven't passed it," he said worriedly to himself.

Finally, he saw the familiar sandy cliff. He dropped to his hands and knees and crawled up to it, not wanting to be visible in case somebody *was* down there. Holding his breath, his eyes scanned the beach below.

It was empty.

Jim let out his breath in something that sounded halfway between a groan and a laugh. "James Robert Howard, you've done it again! You've gone and let your imagination completely run away with you." He was suddenly very relieved that he hadn't shared his suspicions with anybody yet!

He was about a third of the way back down the trail when his foot broke a twig. It cracked loudly, and startled Jim, who had been paying more attention to the thoughts in his head than to the path in front of him.

"What was that?" hissed a voice, about fifteen yards away. "Did you step on something?" Jim froze.

"Nah," said another voice off to the right. "It was probably just a deer or something. These woods are full of 'em. Stop messin' around and finish helping me unroll this hose!"

Jim's breathing suddenly seemed very loud to him. In fact, he was sure that even if he didn't move a muscle, his heart was pounding so loudly it would give him away to whoever was in the woods. He moved off the trail as quietly as he could and crept behind a bush to try to get a better look at what was going on.

Two men, dressed head to toe in black, were handling what looked like a long fire hose, but about three times as wide as any fire hose Jim had ever seen before. One end of the tube was attached to a truck that was parked in a clearing about 250 yards from the water, and the two men were unrolling the rest of it down to the beach. Fascinated, Jim kept watching, wondering what they were up to. He didn't have to wait long.

"I told you we should have started this earlier, Dad!" hissed the first voice Jim had heard. "By the time we get this down to the beach and pump out the stuff in the truck, this job will have taken a couple of hours – that's too long!"

"Well, Frank, why don't you shut your trap, get to work, and maybe we can speed it along?" The other voice sounded really irritated. "We stand to earn a whole lot of money if we do this job, so quit your complainin' and let me do the thinking!"

Jim's head was spinning. He had been right in his guess about the Conners being involved – this had to be the same Frank and Mr. Conner that Mrs. Forrest had mentioned.

"I wonder what they're talking about – why did they say 'pumping' instead of 'dumping'?" Jim wondered. The truck in the clearing was actually a large tanker. "They must have used one of the old forest service roads to get it up here," he decided, wondering why they had chosen that kind of truck. If anything, he would have expected to see something that looked more like a dump truck – after all, wouldn't that be the sensible thing to use to carry up things like the old cans and other garbage he'd seen at the beach?

"Well, Dad," snarled Frank, "I think that it would have been much smarter to build in some extra time for this trial run. Maybe next time you'll listen to me!"

"Well, Mr. Big Mouth, we don't have extra time, do we? We have to get this pumped in before that big storm hits later tonight. If we don't, that stuff will just be floating around here for some busybody to find, and then we won't get our bonus," Mr. Conner said, sounding totally fed up. "But, if we handle this first job correctly *tonight*, the storm should carry all this out to sea, and no one will be the wiser." He moved away, muttering to himself about what a curse it was for someone as clever as him to have such a stupid, stubborn son.

Why were they acting like this? Was it the first time they had done this? Jim had seen the state of the beach. People, no doubt

Frank and his father, had been dumping garbage there for some time. Jim decided to find out what was in the truck while the Conners were arguing down by the water.

He edged near to where the plastic tube was attached to the big tank. It wasn't tightly sealed, and something black and thick was dripping out. Jim knew immediately what it was. After all, he had helped his dad in the garage before. It was thick, slimy waste oil, and it looked like these two crooks were about to pump it into the bay!

Jim realized that his earlier plan of just collecting evidence was not going to work. He could not stand by and let the Conners get away with this – if that oil went into the bay, it would poison every living thing in the water. He was simply going to have to stop it.

Suddenly, Jim heard raised voices, followed by a scream. He raced over to the trees near the path and peered out. His parents and the Westons, on their way back from their trip to see the stars, had met up with the Conners on the path above the beach, and were now being held at gunpoint!

CHAPTER 8

"I say, you ought to just surrender now," super-spy Cliff Gunn said to his two captors. "For there's no way two characters like yourselves could possibly hope to keep me prisoner for long." He laughed in their faces, slyly undid the last bit of rope around his hands, and paralyzed them with a stun gun hidden in his watch. "I did try to warn you two chaps." Gunn smiled, as their huge bodies fell clumsily to the ground. "Don't you know I find firearms tacky and obvious? I prefer to have a few other tricks up my sleeve." Saying that, he removed a length of thin wire from the seam of his impeccable dinner jacket and securely bound the two criminals. "Well, I must go have a chat with your boss, Dr. Death. It seems he plans to dump poison gas in my country, and we simply can't have that now, can we?" With that, Gunn was gone...

"Pull yourself together, James Robert Howard, this is no time for daydreaming! Why can't you remember the most basic rule of boy scouts?" Jim groaned to himself.

"'Be prepared.' It's so simple – why can't you even manage that?"

He was frantically searching his backpack for something, *anything*, that could help him stop the Conners and save his family and the Westons. "Two comic books, a package of chewing gum, an old battery, a belt, some matchbox cars, my windbreaker, the gross socks I wore into the ocean... the only good things I have are the flashlight and camera, and if I use either one of those, it would give me away in a second!"

Jim knew he had to act fast, but he couldn't think of anything to do – not even his imagination was helping. In the meantime, the Conners were sneering at the four adults they were holding captive.

"Well, a bunch of little nature lovers enjoying a nice nighttime walk," Frank said rudely. "You know, if you guys had waited until summer, like intelligent tourists, you would never have gotten yourselves into this kind of trouble. The only reason we're here tonight is because we were sure nobody would be stupid enough to stay in the park during the rainy season."

"Hey, shut your mouth," Mr. Conner snarled at his son. "Just do your part so we can get out of here before anybody realizes these people are missing!"

"Wha-what are you going to do with us?" Jim's mom asked nervously. "I mean, my little boy is waiting for me at home…"

Jim's dad jumped in. "You know, we haven't seen your faces – why don't you let us go…? We wouldn't be able to identify you. We really need to get back to our son."

"Well, you should have thought about that before you came barging right into the middle of our plan," said Frank. "Like I said, the only reason you're in this sticky situation is because of your own stupidity."

Sticky situation. A sticky situation – the idea popped into Jim's head like a flash. Yes, that Frank obviously thought he was quite a comedian with his cracks about sticky situations. That's exactly what he was going to create when he poured all that thick, gooey oil into the ocean.

But Jim's imagination hadn't let him down. He was going to create his own sticky situation for the Conners. He had had an inspiration – one that could keep the oil out of the bay, *and* save his parents and the Westons at the same time. And best of all, he had everything he needed right with him.

He quietly edged out of his hiding place and back up the path to the truck. He knew he needed to work fast, but if his luck held, and they didn't find him first, he would succeed.

About ten minutes later, the Conners finished preparing the tube down to the ocean, and Frank started the climb back up to the truck to start the oil pumping. Mr. Conner stayed on the beach with the prisoners – exactly what Jim had hoped he would do.

Frank went to the gearbox on the front of the tank and flipped the switch to start pumping the oil out. Nothing happened. He wiggled the wires. Nothing happened. He kicked at the box. Nothing happened.

"Hey," yelled Mr. Conner, from down at the beach, "nothing's coming out – what's going on?"

"There's something that's got the gears all stuck together," Frank shrieked, starting to lose his head.

"Yes, there is," chuckled Jim to himself from his hiding place down the path. "It's a nice chewy piece of chewing gum. Try to get *that* unstuck before morning!" He was busily tying one end of his long hiking boot laces to a tree near the path.

"Well, get down here and guard these people. I'll take care of it, as usual!" yelled Mr. Conner, sounding completely fed up with Frank.

Frank, obeying quickly for once, started running down the path. *WHAM!* He crashed to the ground, having tripped over the bootlace that Jim was holding taut across the path.

Jim was on Frank's back in a flash, pressing his knee into the indentation between Frank's shoulders to keep him down. While Jim fumbled with another bootlace to tie Frank's hands behind his back, Frank started to struggle to get up. Quick as a flash, Jim pulled a dead battery out of his pocket and pressed the circle of cold steel against Frank's neck.

"Freeze!" he hissed, hoping his voice wouldn't sound too young if he whispered. Frank, who was really quite a coward, went limp and started whimpering. "Please don't hurt me," he begged. Jim quickly shut him up by shoving one of his old socks into Frank's mouth.

Jim then finished tying Frank's hands. He couldn't remember one of the official boy scout knots, but he wrapped the wrists so tightly, and tied so many double knots, that he didn't think Frank would be able to get loose. He then propped Frank up against a nearby tree and laced his spare belt through Frank's elbows and around the trunk. He moved around to inspect his work, making sure Frank was secure.

When Frank saw how young his captor was, he started to squirm and kick, but he couldn't budge. Nor could he make a sound – Jim's old sock was certainly doing the trick!

Jim leaned over Frank and whispered, "If you think *that* tastes bad, just think of what the poor animals in the bay would have thought if you had poured in all that oil! It serves you right!"

Jim would have loved to stay and gloat, but he had more work to do. He grabbed his backpack and moved down the path toward the beach, stumbling slightly in his unlaced boots.

When he reached the trees at the edge of the beach, he saw that he was starting to run out of time. Mr. Conner was starting to get very anxious. "FRANK!" he bellowed, forgetting his need to keep their identities secret. "Frank! What are you doing up there?"

Jim hurriedly climbed one of the trees overhanging the path and set to work. Just as he was finishing, he shifted his weight to give one final tug to his handiwork, and started to slip.

The loud snap of branches as he frantically tried to catch himself rang out across the beach like a shot. Mr. Conner grabbed Jim's mom by the arm and yanked her up. "Come with me," he hissed at her, and started dragging her up the beach, his gun pointed at her side. "Who's there?" he called up, a dangerous edge sounding in his voice.

Jim knew he was going to have to give himself up, or else Mr. Conner might think it was the police, and then his mom would *really* be in danger.

"Mom?" Jim called, stumbling out of the forest, trying to look as lost and confused as possible. "Is my mom down here?"

Mr. Conner started to laugh, and shoved Jim's mom back over to the other three adults. "Hey, come here, kid." He smiled wickedly at Jim. "What are you doing out at this time of night?"

Jim walked up as innocently as he could. He had to get Mr. Conner to chase him over to the big tree. His mind was racing furiously to come up with a plan.

"Jim, do what he says," his dad called out, "it'll be OK. Just do what he says, and then come over here by us." Jim looked over at his parents and saw that his mom was crying.

"I know, Dad," he said, trying to make his smile as reassuring as possible. "Everything *will* be OK." He had thought of a way that his plan could still work. He kept walking up to Mr. Conner.

Then, when he was about fifteen feet away, he suddenly whipped out the camera. Closing his eyes against the bright flash, he quickly snapped a picture of Mr. Conner, and then turned, running as fast as he could back up to the path.

"I hope the flash blinded him too much to shoot," Jim prayed to himself as he ran. He heard Mr. Conner's footsteps in the sand behind him.

"You rotten kid! Get back here – you know I'm going to catch you, and then I'm really going to let you have it!"

Mr. Conner was panting behind him. There it was! Jim saw the white flag in the tree and raced for it with all his might. His heart was pounding in his chest. He was almost there...

Then, his luck ran out. His unlaced boot started to come off in the sand, he tripped, and went down!

Mr. Conner was on him in a flash. "Hey kid," he wheezed, "what's the matter with you – you got something stuck in your ears?" He jerked Jim up roughly by the shoulder. "Give me that camera! What were you running over here for?" He had seen the flash of white in the tree as well. "This? You were running for this? It's just a smelly old sock!"

Mr. Conner reached up and impatiently jerked at the sock to pull it out of the tree. The sock, which had been tied in a quick-release knot over the branch, shot out of his hand, and the weight it had been supporting – a backpack filled with rocks – swung down and crashed into Mr. Conner's head.

Mr. Conner fell to the ground, unconscious. Jim saw his gun lying a few feet from his hand, and, not wanting to touch it, covered it with some rocks so that Mr. Conner wouldn't find it if he suddenly came to.

Then he turned and raced back to the beach to see if everybody was all right. He found that his dad had worked himself free and was running up the beach toward the path. His mom and the Westons were frantically trying to get their own hands untied so they could come and help as well.

"It's all right!" yelled Jim, jumping up

and down with excitement. "I told you it was all right! I took care of both of them!" He couldn't say any more because his dad was squeezing him too tightly.

"Come on, Dad," said Jim, starting to get embarrassed, "we don't have time for this. I think we should probably go and tie up Mr. Conner, and make sure Frank hasn't escaped."

"How do you know their names?" demanded his father. "Who are these people, and what are you doing out here in the middle of all this?" His mom and the Westons, who had just run up, joined in and started clamoring for information.

"You wouldn't believe *how* much I know about all this," began Jim, motioning for quiet. "But I really think we better make sure that these two are secure. Then," he smiled coolly, "let's go back to the cabin so we can let Mrs. Forrest know everything's OK, and call the police. They're probably going to want to go and have a little chat with the ringleader of this scheme, a certain Mr. Otto Farnsworth. Trust me, I'm on top of this situation."

CHAPTER 9

The conquering hero had returned, victorious! He sank back into the car's plush upholstery, completely exhausted by his ordeal, but too exhilarated to sleep. The events of the past several days ran through his mind over and over again – visions of the lives he had saved, the crime ring he had destroyed. He had gone into the battle knowing the desperate need for him to succeed, but he had surprised even himself with his courage and cunning. "You know," the hero thought to himself, "all you need to win in this game is a little imagination." He got out of the car where the mayor was waiting for him in the middle of the town. The mayor smiled respectfully at the hero and asked, "How did you figure out who was behind all these dastardly deeds, and how in the world did you know how to stop them?"

James Robert Howard thought for a moment before answering. "Well, Mr. Mayor, I guess the answers were all right there in my mind the whole time – all I had to do was pay attention." He turned around and grinned at his parents and the Westons who were standing a few feet away.

The mayor started to laugh and slapped him on the back. "Well, we all feel real lucky that a boy with your kind of imagination and style was around to help save our coastline – thanks for your hard work, son!"

Later, as Jim rode back to the cabin with his parents and the Westons, he filled them in on the details they had missed during all the excitement the night before. He told them the whole story, starting with when he had found the trapped sea lion.

"Jim, what I want to know is what you were doing for so long in that interrogation room at the police station," his dad asked. "The officers said they wanted you to help them break one of the suspect's stories."

Jim smothered a giant yawn – he had not had any rest since the day before, when he had fallen asleep on the beach after his swim. "Well, they really did need my help. You see, I had overheard everything the Conners were saying on the beach, so I was able to let the cops know whenever they started lying.

"Oh boy," he laughed, "you should have seen their faces when the police told them they knew all about their scheme with Otto Farnsworth to start dumping that gooey oil sludge into the ocean. I thought old Frank was going to start crying right there!

"Then, when they brought in Mr. Farnsworth, it really got good. He threatened to sue everybody in the town for false arrest, until Frank started blubbering about how the cops knew the whole story. Mr. Farnsworth turned bright red and started spluttering – I thought he was going to explode for sure!" Jim sat back in his seat. "I'm really glad they let me stay and see how it all turned out."

Jim's mom turned around in her seat to look at him. "Well, we couldn't be more proud of what you did out there, Jim. I guess you're the real adventurer out of all of us!"

"Adventurer!" burst out Mr. Weston, "doggone it, he's more than that – this here boy's an honest-to-goodness hero! We're all going to have one heck of a time keepin' *him* entertained for the rest of this trip. What should we plan next? A roundup of wild buffalo? A deep-sea diving expedition? Boy, what's your pleasure? You deserve the vacation of your life!"

But Mr. Weston got no answer. James Robert Howard, the great adventurer, had fallen sound asleep.

TITLES IN THE SERIES

SET 9A

Television Drama
Time for Sale
The Shady Deal
The Loch Ness Monster Mystery
Secrets of the Desert

SET 9B

To JJ From CC
Pandora's Box
The Birthday Disaster
The Song of the Mantis
Helping the Hoiho

SET 9C

Glumly
Rupert and the Griffin
The Tree, the Trunk, and the Tuba
Errol the Peril
Cassidy's Magic

SET 9D

Barney
Get a Grip, Pip!
Casey's Case
Dear Future
Strange Meetings

SET 10A

A Battle of Words
The Rainbow Solution
Fortune's Friend
Eureka
It's a Frog's Life

SET 10B

The Cat Burglar of Pethaven Drive
The Matchbox
In Search of the Great Bears
Many Happy Returns
Spider Relatives

SET 10C

Horrible Hank
Brian's Brilliant Career
Fernitickles
It's All in Your Mind,
    James Robert
Wing High, Gooftah

SET 10D

The Week of the Jellyhoppers
Timothy Whuffenpuffen-
    Whippersnapper
Timedetectors
Ryan's Dog Ringo
The Secret of Kiribu Tapu Lagoon